WITHDRAWN

DATE DUE

D0859267

Football Superstars

By Jim Gigliotti

The
Child's
World®
www.childsworld.com

Published in the United States of America by The Child's World®
P.O. Box 326 • Chanhassen, MN 55317-0326
800-599-READ • www.childsworld.com

ACKNOWLEDGMENTS

The Child's World®: Mary Berendes, Publishing Director

Produced by Shoreline Publishing Group LLC
President / Editorial Director: James Buckley, Jr.
Designer: Tom Carling, carlingdesign.com
Cover Art: Slimfilms
Copy Editor: Beth Adelman

Photo Credits
All photos by Robbins Photography (www.robbinsphoto.net)

LIBRARY OF CONGRESS CATALOGING-IN-PUBLICATION DATA

Gigliotti, Jim.
  Football superstars / by Jim Gigliotti.
     p. cm. — (Boys rock!)
  Includes bibliographical references and index.
  ISBN 1-59296-730-2 (library bound : alk. paper)
  1. Football players—United States—Biography—Juvenile
literature. I. Title. II. Series.
  GV939.A1G53 2006
  796.332092'2—dc22

                              2006001635

CONTENTS

4 CHAPTER 1

The Field Generals

14 CHAPTER 2

Head for
the End Zone!

24 CHAPTER 3

Heavy
Hitters

30 GLOSSARY

31 FIND OUT MORE

32 INDEX

THE FIELD
Generals

If you've picked up this book, chances are you're a football fan. Maybe everyone in your family is a fan, too, along with lots of your friends. It's no surprise if they are—the National Football League (NFL) is the most popular league in the United States. The NFL's championship game, the Super Bowl, is the most popular one-day event in all of sports.

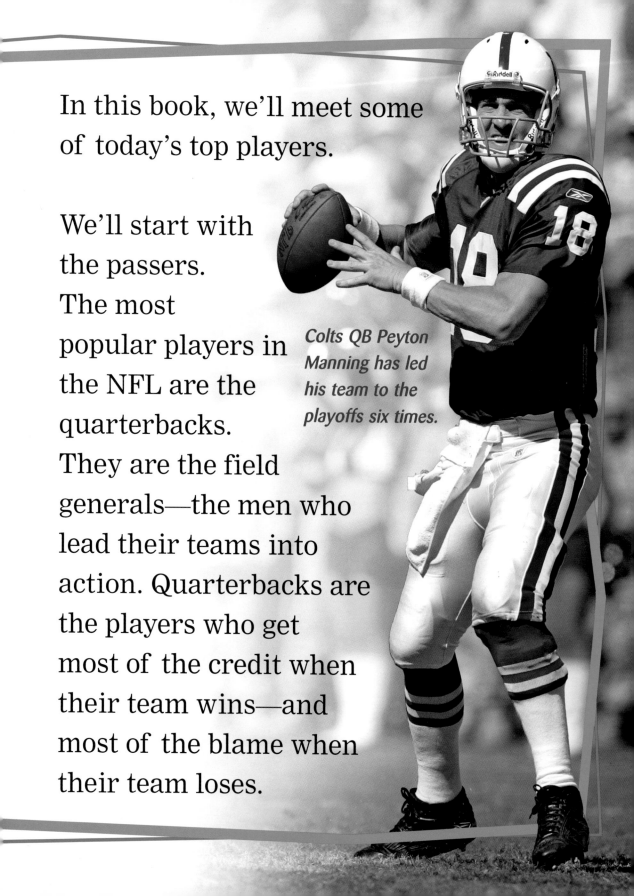

In this book, we'll meet some of today's top players.

We'll start with the passers. The most popular players in the NFL are the quarterbacks.

Colts QB Peyton Manning has led his team to the playoffs six times.

They are the field generals—the men who lead their teams into action. Quarterbacks are the players who get most of the credit when their team wins—and most of the blame when their team loses.

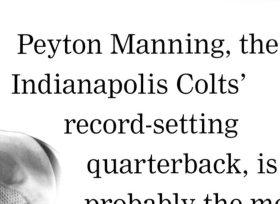

Peyton Manning, the Indianapolis Colts' record-setting quarterback, is probably the most famous player in the NFL right now. In 2004, he threw 49 touchdown passes in one season—more than any other player in league history.

Like father, like son: Peyton's dad, Archie, was a longtime NFL quarterback.

Peyton is one of the NFL's smartest players. He often goes up to the **line of scrimmage**, takes a look at the defense, and changes the play with an **audible**.

His quick feet and calm attitude make him difficult to **sack**. And with his quick hands, he can often throw a pass before the defense has a chance to get to him.

David Carr of the Houston Texans holds the record for being sacked the most times in one season. He was sacked 176 times in 2003. Ouch!

Peyton came to the NFL as the number-one pick in the 1998 **draft**. Since then, he has made the Colts winners.

All in the Family

Peyton is just one of the quarterbacks in the Manning family. His younger brother Eli is a budding superstar for the New York Giants. Eli led his team to the playoffs in 2005.

Green Bay Packers quarterback Brett Favre combines toughness and leadership with a strong right arm. Led by Brett, the Packers won Super Bowl XXXI and the 1996 NFL **title**.

Brett has been named to the NFL's all-star game—the Pro Bowl—seven times.

Brett is always there for his team, too. Through 2005, he had started in 240 straight games—by far the most for any quarterback in the NFL.

Packers fans know that no game is out of reach when Brett has the ball in his hands. That's the same way New England Patriots fans feel about their quarterback, Tom Brady.

Tom Brady was just 24 years old when he led his team to his first Super-Bowl win.

Tom has quickly become known as one of the NFL's best **comeback artists**. He led the Patriots' game-winning drive in Super Bowl XXXVI after the 2001 season. He also led the Patriots to 2003 and 2004 NFL titles.

Many of today's young quarterbacks can beat teams with their feet as well as with their arms. Michael Vick of the Atlanta Falcons is at the top of the list of these running quarterbacks. Michael is a left-handed passer. He's also a dazzling runner with the speed of a sprinter and the moves of the best running backs.

In only his second season, Michael led the Falcons to the 2002 playoffs. After missing much of 2003 with injuries, he came back full-time in 2004. That season, he led the Falcons to the NFC Championship Game—just one win away from the Super Bowl.

A fearsome sight: Michael Vick looking downfield with room to run!

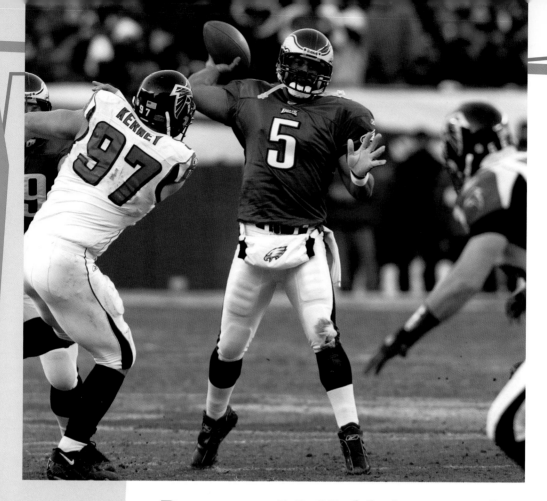

Donovan McNabb has led his team to four NFC Championship Games.

Donovan McNabb is one of pro football's great leaders. In his career with the Philadelphia Eagles, which began in 1999, Donovan has shown lots of skills. He can use his strong arm to throw touchdown passes. He can run well, and he can lead his team. McNabb will do whatever it takes to help the Eagles win. Since McNabb arrived, the team has won more games than any other team in its **conference**. They also won the 2004 NFC championship.

Who's Next?

If you're looking for the NFL's next great superstar quarterback, it might be the Cincinnati Bengals' Carson Palmer (right), who had an exciting season in 2005. Or it might be Ben Roethlisberger of the Pittsburgh Steelers, whose team won Super Bowl XL. Or maybe it will be someone from your school!

2

HEAD FOR THE
End Zone!

Winning a football game comes down to scoring more points than the other team. "Gamebreakers" are the guys who put the ball in the end zone more than any other players in the sport.

Speedy and durable San Diego Chargers running back LaDainian Tomlinson is at the top of that list. In one stretch of 18 games in 2004 and 2005, LaDainian scored at least one touchdown in every game he played. That tied the longest streak in NFL history.

OPPOSITE PAGE
NFL players always stretch their muscles before they play. Here's LaDainian (known as "LT") getting ready for another game.

In 2003, Kansas City Chiefs running back Priest Holmes set an NFL record by scoring 27 touchdowns. This broke the record set by the Rams' Marshall Faulk just three years earlier. In 2004, Priest scored 15 touchdowns—even though he played in only half of the Chiefs' games because of an injury!

Quarterbacks and running backs start each play from the backfield— the area right behind the line of scrimmage.

Running backs can also catch passes, and Priest is almost as good at receiving as he is at running. His ability to catch passes coming out of the **backfield** helped the

Chiefs of the early 2000s develop one of the most powerful offensive attacks in NFL history.

Priest Holmes has speed, but it's his tough, strong running that has made him a star.

The Seattle Seahawks' Shaun Alexander is tough to defend against. He can pound the ball along the middle of the line of scrimmage, or beat teams with his surprising speed on the outside.

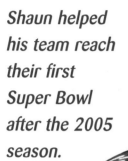

Shaun helped his team reach their first Super Bowl after the 2005 season.

Either way, he has a nose for the end zone. In 2005, on his way to winning the NFL **MVP** award, Shaun broke Priest Holmes'

Many fans discovered Shaun Alexander in 2002 after Seattle played the Minnesota Vikings. The Seahawks beat the Vikings 48–23, with Shaun scoring five touchdowns—all before halftime! That set a record for the most touchdowns in a half.

record by scoring 28 touchdowns in one season.

Shaun also set an NFL record when he ran for 10 or more touchdowns in five straight seasons. In 2004, Shaun's 20 touchdowns set a Seahawks record— but the record only lasted one season!

A wide receiver might have only a few chances to get the football in each game. Still, the best at this position can change the game with a big play. Randy Moss of the Oakland Raiders makes the most of his chances.

Happy Thanksgiving!

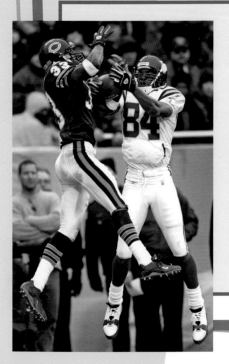

In 1998, Minnesota played the Dallas Cowboys on Thanksgiving Day. Randy Moss caught three passes. No big deal, right? Well, it *was* a big deal! His catches covered 51, 56, and 56 yards, and all three ended up being touchdowns. The Vikings won the game, 46–36.

Perhaps no other wide receiver strikes fear into another team quite like Randy.

He played his first seven seasons with the Minnesota Vikings before joining the Raiders in 2005. In his first game with his new team, he caught a 73-yard touchdown pass. That's the kind of thing he's done ever since he came into the NFL as a first-round draft pick in 1998.

One of Randy's best skills is his running ability after he catches a pass.

Marvin Harrison of the Indianapolis Colts is a rare blend of speed and smarts. Marvin runs exact **pass routes** and always studies the best way to beat the defender. Sometimes the best way is by turning on the jets to burn past quick defensive backs!

Marvin and quarterback Peyton Manning have played

together on the Colts for 10 years, so each player always seems to know what the other is thinking. In 2005, Marvin and Peyton teamed up to set a career record for the most touchdowns by a quarterback-receiver pair.

All of that makes Marvin one of the top wide receivers in the game today—and in the history of the NFL. He is rapidly joining the list of the league's best pass-catchers ever. With his help, the Colts have had some of the best offenses of all time.

Who's the best pass-catcher ever? Jerry Rice retired in 2005 after having caught a record 1,549 career passes and scoring a record 208 total touchdowns.

3

HEAVY Hitters

The **statistic** that makes a defensive player a star in the NFL is the sack. When a player tackles the opposing quarterback, it can change a game.

In today's NFL, a pair of defensive linemen—the Carolina Panthers' Julius Peppers and the Indianapolis Colts' Dwight Freeney—are two of the top sack producers.

In 2002, Julius had 12 sacks—one of the best seasons ever by a first-year player. In 2004, Dwight led the NFL with 16 sacks.

Ignoring a blocker, Dwight Freeney (number 93) heads toward the quarterback.

Middle linebackers are sort of like the quarterbacks of the defense.

For the Baltimore Ravens, linebacker Ray Lewis dominates the defense. Ray is an all-around star, whether playing against the run, putting pressure on the quarterback, or covering receivers. He was the MVP of Super Bowl XXXV, which Baltimore won after the 2000 season. In 2003, Ray was named the NFL's defensive player of the year.

Ray Lewis plays all his games with powerful emotion as well as football skill.

In 2003, Derrick set an NFL record for linebackers by returning three interceptions for touchdowns.

Derrick Brooks of the Tampa Bay Buccaneers is one of the top linebackers in NFL history. Derrick was the key defensive player in Super Bowl XXXVII after the 2002 season. He led the Buccaneers' defense to victory over Oakland, 48–21.

You might catch a pass against tough-tackling Ed Reed (in white), but you won't get far!

Defensive backs are big-play performers who can change the **pace** of a game with a key interception—or a crunching hit.

Baltimore's Ed Reed did plenty of both in 2004, when he was named the NFL's defensive player of the year.

That season, he led the league with nine interceptions, one of which he returned a record 106 yards for a touchdown.

Pittsburgh's Troy Polamalu brings the force of a linebacker to the safety position. Troy covers receivers, but he has also become one of the league's toughest tacklers. He helped the Steelers win Super Bowl XL.

Proud of his Samoan heritage, Troy hasn't cut his hair in five years!

GLOSSARY

audible a change in a play, called at the line of scrimmage

backfield the area on the field behind the quarterback where the running backs usually line up

comeback artists players known for coming from behind to win a game

conference a group of sports teams that is smaller than a league—for example, the NFL's National Football Conference (NFC) and American Football Conference (AFC)

draft a process by which football teams choose which players they want for the next season

interceptions passes caught by the other team instead of by the intended receivers

line of scrimmage the place on the field where the two teams line up face-to-face, on opposite sides of the ball

MVP abbreviation for Most Valuable Player

pace how quickly or slowly a game is being played

pass routes exact ways receivers are supposed to run on certain plays

sack to tackle a quarterback (or any player who is attempting to pass) behind the line of scrimmage

statistic a number that shows how well or how many times an athlete has done something

title another word for a championship

FIND OUT MORE

BOOKS

America's Greatest Game
  by James Buckley, Jr.
  (Hyperion Books for Children, New York) 1998
  A history of football, from its earliest days to the Super Bowl.

Eyewitness Football
  by James Buckley Jr.
  (Dorling Kindersley, New York) 1999
  A photo-filled book that covers every part of football, from
  equipment to strategy to history.

Michael Vick
  by Jeff Savage
  (Lerner Publications, Minneapolis, MN) 2005
  A biography of this multitalented superstar.

Super Sports Star Peyton Manning
  by Ken Rappoport
  (Enslow Publishers, Berkeley Heights, NJ) 2003
  A biography of one of the league's top players.

WEB SITES

Visit our home page for lots of links about football teams and
  players: www.childsworld.com/links

Note to Parents, Teachers, and Librarians: We routinely check our Web links to
make sure they're safe, active sites—so encourage your readers to check them out!

INDEX

Alexander, Shaun, 18, 19

Atlanta Falcons, 10-11

Baltimore Ravens, 26, 28

Brady, Tom, 9

Brooks, Derrick, 27

Carolina Panthers, 24

Carr, David, 7

Favre, Brett, 8, 9

Freeney, Dwight, 24-25

Green Bay Packers, 8, 9

Harrison, Marvin, 22-23

Holmes, Priest, 16-17, 18

Houston Texans, 7

Indianapolis Colts, 5, 6-7, 22-23, 24

Kansas City Chiefs, 16-17

Lewis, Ray, 26

Manning, Archie, 6

Manning, Eli, 7

Manning, Peyton, 5, 6-7, 22-23

McNabb, Donovan, 12-13

Minnesota Vikings, 19, 20, 21

Moss, Randy, 20-21

New England Patriots, 9

New York Giants, 7

Oakland Raiders, 20-21

Palmer, Carson, 13

Peppers, Julius, 24-25

Philadelphia Eagles, 12-13

Pittsburgh Steelers, 13, 29

Polamalu, Troy, 29

Pro Bowl, 8

Reed, Ed, 28-29

Roethlisberger, Ben, 13

San Diego Chargers, 15

Seattle Seahawks, 18-19

Super Bowl, 4, 9, 11, 18
    Super Bowl XXXI, 8
    Super Bowl XXXV, 26
    Super Bowl XXXVI, 9
    Super Bowl XXXVII, 27
    Super Bowl XL, 13, 29

Tampa Bay Buccaneers, 27

Tomlinson, LaDainian, 15

Vick, Michael, 10-11

Young, Steve, 10

JIM GIGLIOTTI is a writer who lives in southern California with his wife and two children. A former editor with the National Football League's publishing division, he has written more than a dozen books about sports and personalities, including *Stadium Stories: USC Trojans* and *Watching Football* (with former NFL star Daryl Johnston).